Written by Alan Dapré
Illustrated by Igor Sinkovec

Published by Pearson Education Limited, Edinburgh Gate, Harlow, Essex, CM20 2JE.

www.pearsonschools.co.uk

Text © Alan Dapré 2013

Original illustrations © Pearson Education Limited 2013
Illustrated by Igor Sinkovec, Advocate

The right of Alan Dapré to be identified as author of this work has been asserted by him in accordance with the Copyright, Designs and Patents Act 1988.

First published 2013

18
10 9 8 7

British Library Cataloguing in Publication Data
A catalogue record for this book is available from the British Library

ISBN 978 0 435 14375 6

Copyright notice
All rights reserved. No part of this publication may be reproduced in any form or by any means (including photocopying or storing it in any medium by electronic means and whether or not transiently or incidentally to some other use of this publication) without the written permission of the copyright owner, except in accordance with the provisions of the Copyright, Designs and Patents Act 1988 or under the terms of a licence issued by the Copyright Licensing Agency, Saffron House, 6–10 Kirby Street, London EC1N 8TS (www.cla.co.uk). Applications for the copyright owner's written permission should be addressed to the publisher.

Printed in Great Britain by Ashford Colour Press Ltd.

Acknowledgements
We would like to thank Bangor Central Integrated Primary School, Northern Ireland; Bishop Henderson Church of England Primary School, Somerset; Bletchingdon Parochial Church of England Primary School, Oxfordshire; Brookside Community Primary School, Somerset; Bude Park Primary School, Hull; Cheddington Combined School, Buckinghamshire; Dair House Independent School, Buckinghamshire; Glebe Infant School, Gloucestershire; Henley Green Primary School, Coventry; Lovelace Primary School, Surrey; Our Lady of Peace Junior School, Slough; Tackley Church of England Primary School, Oxfordshire; and Twyford Church of England School, Buckinghamshire for their invaluable help in the development and trialling of the Bug Club resources.

Every effort has been made to contact copyright holders of material reproduced in this book. Any omissions will be rectified in subsequent printings if notice is given to the publishers.

Contents

The Mint Choc Touch   Page 4

The Monster Maze   Page 27

The Mint Choc Touch
Chapter One

Rukma Shikari was not having a great holiday. She blamed it on her brother, Raj, who was nuts about the Ancient Greeks ... and nuts for marching them up a steep rocky hill at the crack of dawn!

"There it is!" Raj whooped, pointing to the Parthenon, a spectacular ancient temple perched above the Greek city of Athens.

"Is that it?" said Rukma, drenched in sweat and grumpiness. "All this way to see a crumbling building with no roof?"

Her dad chuckled as he leafed through his guidebook. "You'd look crumbly too if you were more than two thousand years old."

"The temple was built to worship the goddess of wisdom, Athena," gushed Raj, who ate facts for breakfast. "She had a pet owl."

Rukma gave her brainy brother a cool stare. "Well, I'd rather have an ice cream!"

Raj ignored her. "I'm off to find some carvings," he said, and his gangly legs weaved away between the tall temple columns.

"Don't go too far," muttered Dad, not looking up.

Rukma rammed a wilting sun-hat onto her head and then trudged after her brother. After a minute or two, she left Raj to clamber about alone and flopped down wearily in the shimmering shade.

"If I get any hotter I'll melt," she sighed.

Suddenly the air chilled, as if someone had opened a fridge. Rukma glanced up to see a willowy woman dressed in silk. Her long robe glittered in the light, as though it was flecked with gold.

"May I show you around my temple?" A playful smile flickered across the stranger's lips. "This is a truly magical place."

"What's so magical about old chunks of stone?" Rukma sniffed, unimpressed. "I don't need a guide. I just want ice cream. Lots of it!"

Just then Raj re-appeared, skidding over loose stones. The mysterious guide slipped into the shadows, with a shake of her golden hair.

"Hey, Rukma, I found an ice cream stall," said Raj. They raced out of the temple towards a dusty box on wheels, shaded with a faded umbrella. Raj veered off to ask Dad if they could have money for an ice cream, but his sister ran straight on.

Moments later, she was licking a delicious mint choc cone.

"What did Dad say?" she asked when Raj re-appeared.

"We can – but we have to use our own money," he said.

Rukma waved her ice cream in front of his face between greedy licks. "Well *you* can't! This was the last cone left."

Full of triumph and ice cream, Rukma strolled back to Dad with her now gloomy brother in tow. Dad, still studying his guidebook, asked if they wanted to know how the Parthenon was built.

"All I want is more ice cream," said Rukma, gobbling down her last bit of cone.

Before long, Dad was droning on about columns and walls, so Rukma wandered off. She glared at the boring old temple and glimpsed the mysterious guide hovering in the shadows – staring at her.

"If this place is so magical, prove it!" Rukma shouted, wiggling her fingers like a bad magician. "Help me magic up more ice cream!"

Suddenly, from nowhere, an owl screeched and swooped, brushing her hands with its soft feathers. Rukma screeched too. As the bird flapped back to the temple, she shivered and rubbed her fingers. They suddenly felt as cold as icicles.

"Looks like it might rain," said Raj, clambering up beside her. Brooding black clouds were gathering overhead and the sky darkened, sending tourists scampering for the exit.

Rukma shrugged and idly picked up a warm stone. As she turned it in her palm, it turned ice cold. Wide-eyed, Rukma tossed what she was now holding to Raj.

"It's impossible," he said, trembling.

Rukma shook her head in wonder. "It's ice cream!"

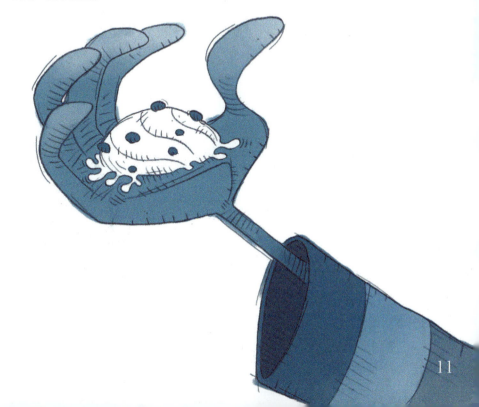

Chapter Two

A second white stone turned green with brown flecks – and very tasty too. Rukma swallowed it greedily and whooped. "It's mint choc, too! Now I can have as much ice cream as I want. Watch this."

She put her arms around a rock and hugged it. Nothing happened. Irritated, Rukma stumbled back, and her fingers bumped the trunk of an olive tree. All at once, she was touching the most delicious tree in the world.

"Cool! I must remember to use just my fingers."

Rukma bit off a leaf and shivered as tasty ice cream slithered down her dry throat. "It's minty chocalicious!" she spluttered.

"We ought to tell Dad," said Raj, feeling suddenly uneasy.

"No way. This is fun!" shouted Rukma, eagerly turning bushes and signposts soft and green.

The clouds parted briefly and Raj glimpsed golden sunlight. Something plopped on to his cap. Glancing up, he saw another drop of ice cream fall from an olive branch.

The tree was starting to melt. Raj broke into a run after Rukma, shouting "Stop!"

It was a good thing that the threat of rain had sent the other tourists packing. Rukma was zipping about, touching everything within reach. Bicycles became icicles. Raj became worried.

He tried to tell Dad all about Rukma's new ice-cream-making ability. Dad just tut-tutted sympathetically, deep in his guidebook, and told Raj to stay out of the sun.

"Tell your sister to do the same, or she'll get sunstroke too."

The thought of Rukma stroking the sun and dooming the whole planet to icy oblivion made Raj shiver. He was glad it was millions of miles away.

Rukma patted a tumbledown wall. An icy blast shot through her fingers into the stone.

"You shouldn't have touched that," shouted Raj, running up.

"It was ruined anyway!"

Raj waved his mobile phone, tempted to call the police. Rukma grabbed it from him and jabbed a button.

"It's the world's first mint choc mobile!"

"That's enough," warned Raj. "You're out of control!" But it wasn't enough for Rukma. She shot him a chilling glance.

"Next stop … the Parthenon!"

Raj was getting desperate. "Can't you see you're changing?"

"So is this temple!" Rukma cackled with glee.

Seeing his sister reach out to touch the temple, Raj sprang forward and grabbed her wrist. Rukma spun and pushed him away with her free hand.

And that was when it happened. Raj froze. His body crackled – and horror hardened on his face.

Rukma stopped. Then she staggered away and dropped to her knees.

"What have I done?"

Raj didn't answer. He was frozen at an impossible angle. An ice cream statue!

Above Rukma's head, a blanket of cloud broke apart and rays of dazzling sunlight struck the temple. She stared sadly at Raj, who seemed to be crying. A fat drip rolled down his cheek. No, wait ... not crying.

Melting!

More drops fell from her brother's peaked hat. "Your hat is melting!" shrieked Rukma. She dragged him across the shimmering sand, into the cool temple shadows.

Just in time!

The last wisp of cloud evaporated in the rising heat and left a clear blue sky behind. Somewhere in the hot city below, a clock struck noon.

Chapter Three

"I'm so sorry, Raj," Rukma sobbed, petrified with fear. "I wish everything were normal again."

She backed away from her brother – straight into Dad, who was still reading. A single tingling finger brushed his wrist and released its terrible minty magic.

"No!" shouted Rukma.

Dad said nothing. Now two ice cream statues stood in the grim shadow of the temple.

"What have I done?" Rukma wailed.

"Greed does terrible things," said a bitterly cold voice. The guide was back, floating soundlessly up the steps of the temple. "You are not the first. And you will not be the last!"

"Make the magic stop," Rukma begged, holding up her fingers. She ran towards the guide, who enveloped her in her billowing white robe.

"Open your eyes," whispered the guide. The air was warm and still. Rukma looked around. Water dripped from the roof of a dark, dank cave.

"Where are we?" she asked drowsily.

"This way," said the guide, gesturing to a narrow passage. They walked until they came to a trickling spring. "Kneel and wash."

Rukma stared at her magical fingers, so cold that they hurt.

"If I touch this water, it will become sludge," she groaned.

"This is my magic spring," whispered the guide, as she gestured for Rukma to wash in the bubbling pool. Rukma dipped in both hands. She gasped as ice cream streamed from her fingertips and melted away in the clear spring water.

An owl fluttered alongside and cocked its head, as if asking a question. Rukma knew there was only one answer.

"I'll never be greedy again," she muttered, wiser now. "I promise."

Chapter Four

At last, some warmth flooded Rukma's fingers as the flow of ice cream trickled to nothing. She splashed cool water on her face and stood, refreshed.

"This way," said the guide, leading her back the way they had come. Rukma spied daylight in the distance and wondered what lay outside. Soon she emerged, blinking, into the dazzling sunlight.

Rukma saw the green and brown olive tree first. Green leaves. Brown trunk. Was everything all right? She glanced around and giggled with relief. The bicycles were once again red, the signposts white.

"Everything is how it was," she whispered, feeling joy in her fluttering heart.

"Not everything," said the guide. Her words chilled Rukma. She ran headlong towards the temple shadows, where two statues stood together in the gloom.

"Dad?"

Dad stepped forward, dazed. "Rukma! There you are." He rubbed his glowing forehead. "I've been out in the sun too long. I just had the strangest day-dream."

Rukma glanced at the guide, who smiled and nodded. Rushing forward, Rukma cuddled Dad like a long-lost favourite teddy.

Her brother still faced the other way and hadn't moved.

"Raj?"

Rukma grabbed him around the waist and gave him a big hug, too.

"Get off, you soppy thing!" cried Raj, spinning around.

"You were as still as a statue," she explained, beaming with delight.

"I'm still mad at you," he said, half joking. "My hat's squished and look at my phone. I can't get it working. It's melted!"

Rukma shrugged. "I'm sorry."

She glanced around nervously to see if she was being watched, but the guide had gone.

Phew.

Dad piped up. "Has anyone seen my guidebook?"

"That's melted too," mumbled Rukma under her breath.

Raj glanced at Rukma. "Is everything how it was?"

Rukma remembered the guide's words. "Not everything."

Her brother looked worried.

"Don't worry; it's just that I feel different. Happier."

Dad led the way out of the temple and scrunched to a stop beside a big umbrella. The ice cream stall was back with more icy treats and ready for business. "Does anyone want a mint choc cone?" he offered.

Rukma turned a sickly shade of green, while behind her, a wise owl hooted with laughter.

The Monster Maze
Chapter One

The hotel pool was full of children having fun in the sun. It was a perfect way to end a holiday – but Rukma's dad had other ideas.

"Today we're off to visit the Palace of Knossos," he said, closing his new guidebook. "It's got a brilliant temple."

"Not another one," groaned Rukma.

"Rukma had a meltdown at the last one," teased Raj, her pesky brother.

"According to this guidebook, Knossos is where the beastly Minotaur lurks – prowling a maze of underground passages and waiting to be fed children," Dad added, pulling a scary face.

"That's just a totally made-up legend to get more visitors," grumbled Rukma.

"Actually, a totally made-up story is a myth," said Raj, who knew lots of things, especially how to wind up his sister.

"What's a legend then?" asked Dad.

"Something at the end of your leg," said Rukma, cheeky as ever.

After a short journey across the island of Crete, Dad parked the hire car at Knossos. He and Raj eagerly explored the ancient ruins while Rukma trudged behind.

"This is the amphitheatre," said Raj, waving at a wide open space with stepped seating.

Dad jabbed at a poster. "Good news, you two. Bella Umbrella is singing here today!"

Raj read the poster aloud, "Bella Umbrella is a famous opera singer, visiting the Palace of Knossos on a minor tour."

"On a Minotaur? Minotaurs don't exist," grumbled Rukma.

Dad rubbed his hands eagerly. "Opera is exciting."

Rukma yawned. "Wake me up when she's finished singing."

Ten minutes later there was still no sign of Bella, and the large crowd was chatting restlessly. Dad rummaged in his cool-bag and pulled out some honey and yoghurt.

"If you get peckish during the performance, you know where to come for some authentic Greek food," he announced.

Normal dads bring popcorn, thought Rukma. A drip of sweat rolled down her cheek. "I'm going for a stroll in the shade to cool off," she announced, nudging her brother to come too.

"Me too," added Raj.

"Make it quick or you'll miss the start," warned Dad.

"What are you up to?" asked Raj, as they ran to the nearest ruined building. Rukma jangled the coins in her pocket.

"It's about time I spent my holiday money in a gift shop."

"Good idea," agreed Raj. "There must be one somewhere."

Their footsteps clattered down the twisting steps, but they slowed as they turned a sharp corner.

"It's a dead end," groaned Raj. He leaned against the huge, stone slab that blocked their way. Rukma grumbled. The slab rumbled.

And Raj tumbled into the darkness.

Chapter Two

Raj was gone. There was no sign of him – just a square hole where the slab had tilted up. Rukma gripped a rock to steady herself and stared into the grim gloom, unsure what to do next.

The brittle stone crumbled and made the decision for her. Grip lost, she plunged forward ... and the slab slammed down!

A moment later, she landed on something soft called Raj.

"Nice of you to drop in," he grumbled.

"I came to save you," said Rukma, bending the truth.

"You mean you fell in too," said Raj, bending it back. "We have to get out before Dad goes crazy with worry."

"Turn on your phone," Rukma urged in her best bossy tone. "I lost mine when I fell."

"I can't," said Raj. "You melted it, remember?"

True, but that was another story. They began scrabbling on the dusty floor for the fallen phone. Rukma grabbed something hard and shiny, then let go with a yelp. A startled beetle skittered into a crack in the hard ground.

"I've found it," said Raj, jabbing the ON button. The black brick flickered into life and he rang Dad's number.

Nothing.

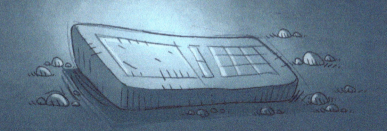

"There's no signal in this miserable dark place," Rukma moaned.

Raj had a thought. "Don't worry, Sis. I've got a bright idea."

Raj pressed the torch function on Rukma's phone and shone the glowing screen at the winding passageway ahead.

"Let's see where this leads," said Rukma, snatching her phone and striding off. Raj ran after her. It was no place to be left behind. Rukma sprinted straight through a spider's web.

"Gross," she spluttered. Raj grinned at his sister's sticky situation. As he helped pull the threads free, a terrible roar wiped the smile off his face.

"Grarrghh!"

"What was that?" he said nervously.

Rukma didn't dare to think. The roar had come from the right, so they darted to the left.

They pounded down dark, winding passages that, according to Dad's guidebook, 'twisted and turned like a prowling black panther'. Before long, the thick walls closed in and they were forced to shuffle sideways.

"Slow down," gasped Raj. Rukma grabbed his hand and dragged him on.

Soon the passage widened and their hurried footsteps clattered noisily in a wide, rocky chamber. A distant roar bounced off the walls and echoed in every direction.

A monstrous groan not far behind got Raj and Rukma thinking about what Dad had told them.

"It's getting louder," groaned Rukma, not daring to say what 'it' might be.

Moments later, something vast thundered into the dusty chamber they had just left. Raj flew off in the opposite direction.

"Don't leave me behind!" yelled Rukma, bolting after him.

Chapter Three

Rukma and Raj desperately searched for a way out of the monster maze.

Minutes passed like hours.

"I'm trapped here forever," muttered Rukma. "With no TV or snacks. Just you!"

"Could be worse."

"What could be worse?" snapped Rukma.

A thunderous roar erupted close by.

"That," said Raj, shuddering.

Desperately, Rukma shone her quivering phone at the wall. The dancing beam shone through a deep crack and she saw a passage.

"What can you see?" asked Raj with his heart thudding.

Rukma gulped as two huge, shadowy horns appeared out of the darkness, accompanied by a dreadful snort. Something vast and frightening sucked air into its lungs and bellowed louder than a herd of bulls. A rising scale of tuneless roars filled the air, followed by a terrifying groan!

"Hurrrrggghhh!"

Raj and Rukma shot off like rockets strapped to rockets ... straight into a dead end. Long ago the stone roof had caved in here and now a heap of broken rubble barred their way.

The beastly roar still rang in their ears as they stumbled towards a junction with yet another passage, unsure if they had been there before.

"Left or right?" puffed Raj.

"Look out!" cried Rukma, seeing a shadowy, horned shape loom above her terrified brother.

"Tell me it's a dream," whispered Raj. But it wasn't.

"It's a nightmare," wailed Rukma. She dropped the phone in fright.

And all went black.

The monstrous thing's throat rattled like marbles in a vacuum cleaner.

"Don't eat us!" cried Raj.

"Or if you do, eat him first," said Rukma, scooping up her phone.

They backed away while Rukma held up her fading light. The battery was almost dead. Two beefy shoulders above her head started to shake, and a gloomy figure slumped to the ground. Loud sobs rent the air.

Rukma thrust her phone forward and gasped, full of relief.

"It's Bella Umbrella!"

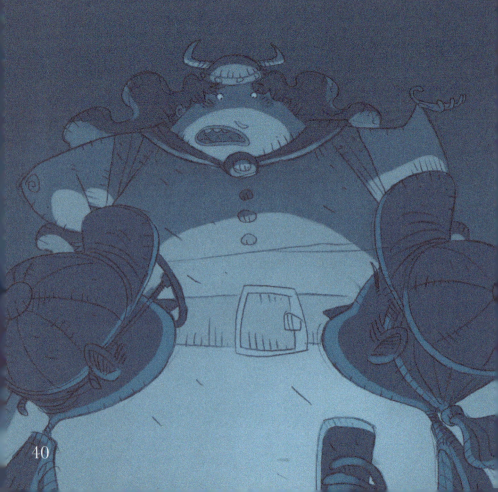

The world famous opera star pawed her throat with a furry glove, while the horned helmet on her head cast pointy shadows on the walls.

"*Mamma mia!* My poor throat is so sore," she snuffled. "The show cannot go on. I cannot sing a note."

The children watched two puffy tonsils jiggle about as she tried to sing in tune.

"Graghh-larghh-laaargh!"

It was not a pretty sight or sound.

"Sounds like you need a big dose of help," said Rukma. A brilliant idea popped into her brain. She shone the light at the chunky stone walls. "But first we must get out of this maze."

Chapter Four

Bella Umbrella puffed down the passage like an old bus and put her brakes on by a dusty sign. "Getting out is simple," she squealed happily.

She sucked in and blew out harder than a hurricane. Dusty, yellow grains swirled all around. When the sandstorm settled, Greek letters were visible.

ΕΧΟΔΟΣ

"The sign says EXIT," Raj yelled. There was even a handy arrow pointing towards a pair of stone pillars. He scampered between them and in an instant was bathed in glorious sunshine.

"Eureka!" he cried.

Rukma skidded into the sunlight of the amphitheatre. She stumbled across Dad sitting on a nearby step, eating honey and yoghurt.

"Stop!" Rukma cried, snatching it from his grasp.

Dad opened his mouth like a bewildered goldfish and stared, baffled, as Rukma vanished back into the shadows.

Raj found Bella Umbrella folded in a sad heap. Rukma got to work mixing the honey and yoghurt together.

"Try this," she urged, waving a spoonful in front of the sobbing singer.

"Everyone is waiting for you to perform outside," said Raj. Bella began to wail. Her mouth opened wide and …

… in went the soothing honey and yoghurt. The two children held their breath while the makeshift medicine went down. Suddenly, Bella sprang to her feet and gobbled what was left in the pot. Her steely eyes shone like lamps and she blasted out a tuneful

"Tra-la-la-la-la-la-lah!"

She skipped in circles, full of delight and yoghurt.

"Who's the best singer in the world?" asked Rukma.

"Me-me-me-me-meeeee," Bella trilled.

"You-you-you-you-youuuu," sang Raj.

Bella gave Rukma a big, squashy squeeze. Her mouth puckered up to give Raj a huge, grateful kiss.

"Time for a quick E X O Δ O Σ," said Raj.

All was quiet when Rukma and Raj sat back down next to Dad.

"You shouldn't have wandered off," Dad said seriously, "or taken my honey and yoghurt!"

"S'pose we got a bit lost and hungry," said Rukma, unsure if Dad would believe the beastly goings on underground.

"Well, you didn't miss anything," added Dad. He tapped his watch and sighed. "There's no sign of Bella Umbrella, so we might as well go."

"Let's stay for a bit," said Rukma, getting herself comfortable.

Dad looked surprised.

A moment later, a mighty roar made them all jump! But this time it came from the crowd as Bella Umbrella hopped and twirled dramatically into the amphitheatre. She opened her lips and sang like a nightingale.

A very big nightingale!

The Shikari family clapped and cheered. Below their feet, a shadowy creature stirred. It raised its horned head and pounded a monstrous fist, keen to be left in peace.

The ground shuddered. Raj shot Rukma a puzzled look.

"Maybe something else is down there?" she said.

And they both shuddered too.